Artists in Their World

Claude Monet

Susie Hodge

FRANKLIN WATTS
LONDON•SYDNEY

This edition 2005

First published in 2002 by
Franklin Watts, 338 Euston Road
London NW1 3BH

Franklin Watts Australia
Hachette Children's Books
Level 17/207 Kent St
Sydney NSW 2000

Series Editor: Adrian Cole
Editor: Sarah Peutrill
Series Designer: Mo Choy
Art Director: Jonathan Hair
Picture Researcher: Diana Morris

A CIP catalogue record for this book
is available from the British Library.

ISBN 0 7496 6625 0

Dewey Classification Number 759.4

Printed in China

Acknowledgments

AKG London: fr cover br,10tr, 16t, 16b, 17b, 30tr, 34bl.   Bibliothèque Nationale, Paris: AKG London fr cover
bl.   Branger-Viollet: 24tl.   British Library: Bridgeman 36tr.   Britstock-IFA: 12tl.   Deutsches Museum, Munich:
AKG London 31br.   Mary Evans PL: 31t.   J Paul Getty Museum, Malibou: Bridgeman 40b.   David Gurr/Eye
Ubiquitous: 26tl.   Robert Holmes/Corbis: 28cl, 41bl.   Wolfgang Kaehler/Corbis: 22tr.   Erich Lessing/AKG
London: 10bl, 22bl.   Michael Maslan Historic Photos/Corbis: 20tr.   Musée Marmottan, Paris: AKG London
8tr; 39 ©ADAGP, Paris and DACS, London 2002 : Giraudon/Bridgeman 21 ©ADAGP, Paris and DACS,
London 2002.   Musée D'Orsay, Paris: Bridgeman 13 &19 ©ADAGP, Paris and DACS, London 2002 :
Giraudon/Bridgeman 33 ©ADAGP, Paris and DACS, London 2002 : Erich Lessing/AKG London 29 ©ADAGP,
Paris and DACS, London 2002; 43cr:Peter Willi/Artothek 35 ©ADAGP, Paris and DACS, London 2002.
Musée du Petit Palais, Geneva: Erich Lessing/AKG London 26c.   Museo de Arte, Sao Paulo: Bridgeman: 9.
Museum Boymans van Beuningen, Rotterdam: Giraudon/Bridgeman 24bc ©ADAGP, Paris and DACS, London
2002.   © National Gallery, London: fr cover c & 25 ©ADAGP, Paris and DACS, London 2002: Bridgeman 15
©ADAGP, Paris and DACS, London 2002.   National Gallery of Art, Washington DC: Lauros-
Giraudon/Bridgeman 27 ©ADAGP, Paris and DACS, London 2002.   Neue Pinakothek, Munich: Bridgeman
18bl.   Norton Simon Foundation, Pasadena, Ca: 11 ©ADAGP, Paris and DACS, London 2002.   Gianni Dagli
Orti/Corbis: 18tl.   Private Collection: AKG London 14tr, 30bl:Bridgeman 8bl: Photo Archives Matisse 41tr ©
Sucession H Matisse/DACS 2002: Roger-Viollet /Bridgeman fr cover bc, 38bl, 38tr.   Private Collection Tokyo:
Peter Willi/Artothek 37 ©ADAGP, Paris and DACS, London 2002.   © Photo RMN-Michèle Bellot:7t
©ADAGP, Paris and DACS, London 2002.   Sammlung Gaetano Marzotto: AKG London 14cl.   The Savoy
Group: 34c.   Stadelsches Kunstinstitut, Frankfurt: Artothek 12cr ©ADAGP, Paris and DACS, London 2002.
Tate Picture Library: 28tr.   Alan Towse/Ecoscene/Corbis: 6.   Trumler/AKG London: 32tl.   Collection Viollet,
Paris: 20bl.   Staffan Widstrand/Corbis: 32br.   Adam Woolfit/Corbis: 36bl.

Whilst every attempt has been made to clear copyright
should there be any inadvertent omission please apply
in the first instance to the publisher regarding rectification.

Contents

Who was Claude Monet?

Claude Monet was one of the greatest artists of his, or any, time. His paintings have changed the way people view the world and his style is famous around the world. Today thousands of items – biscuit tins, mouse mats, tablecloths – are printed with his distinctive images. It seems people cannot get enough of his work!

EARLY LIFE

Oscar-Claude was born in Paris on 14 November 1840. He lived with his parents and older brother Léon in a small apartment, near the River Seine. His family called him Oscar but he was to become famous as Claude Monet.

The family did not have much money. When Monet was five, they moved to a house near Le Havre in Normandy so Claude's father could work in his brother-in-law's grocery business. After that, their financial situation improved and Claude grew up in comfortable surroundings.

▲ The port of Le Havre, France, where Monet spent most of his childhood. This photograph was taken before the Second World War, during which many of Le Havre's buildings were damaged.

BY THE SEA

Monet had a happy home life. There was a lot to see and do around the bustling port. He loved the fresh air and the sea and spent a lot of time on the beach and in the surrounding countryside. At school, his art teacher encouraged him and he filled sketchbooks with drawings of boats, landscapes and people. He also drew caricatures of his teachers, which were popular with his friends!

TIMELINE ▶

14 November 1840	1845	1856	January 1857	January 1858	May 1858	February 1859
Monet is born to Louise-Justine and Adolphe Monet at 45, Rue Laffitte, Paris.	The Monet family moves to Le Havre.	Monet begins drawing caricatures and views of Le Havre.	Monet's mother, Louise-Justine, dies.	Monet's caricatures are on sale in a framer's shop.	Monet meets Eugène Boudin.	Monet moves to Paris and begins working at the Académie Suisse.

LEAVING SCHOOL

When he was 17, Monet's mother died. That same year, he left school. His father's sister, Aunt Marie-Jeanne, looked after him. Seeing his artistic talent she suggested he took drawing lessons, but he much preferred drawing caricatures.

Soon they were on display in a local picture-framer's shop window. Passers-by would gather to admire the pictures and to buy them for a few francs each.

Monet might have carried on like this, but the artist Eugène Boudin (1824-98), who exhibited paintings in the same shop, encouraged Monet to paint in the open air using oil paints. At the time most landscape artists painted in their studios.

▲ Most of Monet's caricatures are amusing drawings of recognisable people – although this one looks rather scary!

STUDYING IN PARIS

On Boudin's advice, Monet went to Paris in 1859 to study art seriously. His father was not enthusiastic, so Aunt Marie-Jeanne helped to pay for it. In Paris, Monet visited art galleries and artists' studios. A successful artist, Constant Troyon (1810-65), said that he had potential, so Monet's father was persuaded to pay for his studies. But he wanted Monet to have 'proper' lessons with exams, while Monet preferred to enrol at the Académie Suisse, which did not follow formal methods of art teaching.

NORTHERN FRANCE

Monet was brought up at a place called Sainte-Adresse, next to Le Havre, at the mouth of the River Seine where it meets the English Channel. The immediate area is called Seine Maritime, and is part of Normandy.

The port of Le Havre is almost square with tall, colourful buildings and lots of boats bobbing on the sea. From the very beginning Monet loved the water. Behind the port, lush green hills rise up above the houses.

The surrounding countryside is full of farms and ancient Norman buildings of grey and beige stone. Monet was fascinated by the way the sun shone on this cold stone, turning it all the colours of the rainbow.

Throughout his life Monet visited places in Northern France, each one with its own attractions that inspired him to paint.

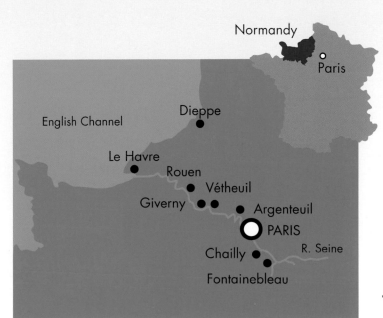

Normandy

Paris

English Channel

Dieppe

Le Havre

Rouen

Vétheuil

Giverny

Argenteuil

PARIS

R. Seine

Chailly

Fontainebleau

Beginnings

Monet was lively and intelligent and made friends easily. After painting all day, he enjoyed sitting in one of the many cafés of Paris, chatting to other artists and writers. But in 1861, he was conscripted to be a soldier in the French army and left Paris for Algeria in North Africa.

Within a year, he became ill and was sent home to Le Havre. Once more, Aunt Marie-Jeanne looked after him. As he recovered, he started painting again in the open air with Boudin and another new friend, the Dutch painter Johan Barthold Jongkind (1819-91). Jongkind taught Monet many ideas, such as painting the same subject in different lights.

'From that time on Jongkind was my true master. I owe to him the final development of my painter's eye.'

Claude Monet

▲ *Monet in his Algerian Soldier's Uniform,* Charles-Marie Lhuillier, 1861. Monet loved the bright uniform and the colour and light he found in Algeria. He thought that being a soldier was a bit of an adventure!

◄ *Evening, Le Havre,* Eugène Boudin, 1866. Boudin was a great influence on Monet's work and shared his passion for nature. Through Boudin, Monet discovered painting 'en plein-air' which means in the open air, directly in front of the subject, rather than in a studio.

TIMELINE ▶			
July 1861	**1862**	**30 October 1862**	**Late November 1862**
Monet is called up for military service.	Monet falls ill and returns to Le Havre.	Monet meets Johan Jongkind. Together with Eugène Boudin, they go on outdoor painting trips.	Monet returns to Paris and enters Charles Gleyre's Academy. He meets Auguste Renoir, Alfred Sisley and Frédéric Bazille.

BECOMING A PROFESSIONAL

Meanwhile, Monet's family were worrying about his lifestyle. Aunt Marie-Jeanne thought that his painting was leading nowhere. In response Monet agreed to try to become a 'professional' artist. In November 1862, when he was almost 22, he returned to Paris and enrolled as a pupil in the studio of the commercial artist, Charles Gleyre.

DEVELOPING A NEW STYLE

Monet still found it hard to keep to the rules. When he was told to make everything perfect, he would not, preferring to paint the scene as he saw it. When Charles Gleyre became ill, Monet began painting exactly as he liked. At the same studio were three other painters, Auguste Renoir (1841-1919), Alfred Sisley (1839-99) and Frédéric Bazille (1841-70). All shared the same views about art. They painted using quick brushstrokes, capturing colour and light. Never before had the accepted way to paint been so challenged.

PAINTING OUTDOORS

The four friends began going on painting trips. Bazille wrote to his mother: 'I have spent eight days at the little village of Chailly near the Forest of Fontainebleau. I was with my friend Monet from Le Havre, who is rather good at landscapes. He gave me some tips that helped me a lot.'

▲ *Jules Le Coeur in the Forest of Fontainebleau*, Auguste Renoir, 1866. Renoir enjoyed the painting trips he made with Monet, Sisley and Bazille to this forest near Paris. Here they could all paint in the way they preferred.

MONEY PROBLEMS

Although Monet and his friends were excited about their new way of painting, many others, including Monet's father, disapproved. Adolphe Monet was still disappointed that his son was not studying at Paris's official art school. He cut off Monet's allowance, which gave Monet money problems throughout the 1860s.

First successes

Paris in the 1860s was an exciting place for a young art student. After work, ideas were shared in cafés with other artists and writers. Monet and his circle of friends frequented the Brasserie des Martyrs and the Guerbois Café.

THE SALON

Each year, an exhibition of living artists' works, called the Salon, was held in Paris. Members of the French Academy of Fine Arts selected the works to be exhibited. Artists' reputations were greatly boosted by having their paintings chosen. Thousands of pictures were entered and many were rejected, some just for being too 'modern'.

In 1863, so many paintings were turned down that artists protested. Napoleon III, then emperor of France, arranged a separate exhibition of refused works in rooms nearby.

▲ *Café Procope*, Von Eugène-André Champollion, 1870. Monet and his friends would fill all the tables at a café like this and have lively conversations about their art.

▲ *Four Hours at the Salon*, François Biard, 1847. Visitors crowded in to see the paintings at the Salon – a bit like we go to see new films at the cinema!

FAMILY DISAPPROVAL

In 1865, Monet met Camille Doncieux, an artists' model, and fell in love. This increased the tensions with his family, since they believed she was not good enough for him.

Despite these family problems Monet continued to develop his style of art, painting things as he saw them and rejecting the traditional rules. This developing style can be seen in *The Mouth of the Seine at Honfleur* (right).

In 1866, Monet entered three paintings for the Salon – *The Mouth of the Seine at Honfleur* and two others, including one of Camille Doncieux. To Monet's surprise and delight, all three works were accepted.

TIMELINE ▶

May 1863	July 1864	1865	15 January 1866	April 1866
The 'Salon des Refusés' shows works by artists rejected by the official Salon.	Charles Gleyre's Academy closes.	Monet shares a studio with Bazille. He meets Camille Doncieux.	Monet leaves the studio shared with Bazille and rents a studio at 1 Place Pigalle, Paris. Here he paints a picture of Camille Doncieux for the Salon.	Monet learns that the Salon has accepted three of his paintings, including the one of Camille.

The Mouth of the Seine at Honfleur, 1865

oil on canvas 88 x 148 cm Norton Simon Museum, California

**Monet painted this on one of his open air painting trips with his friend, Frédéric Bazille.
It shows his love of the sea and fresh air – you can almost feel the spray from the waves!**

*'Gradually my eyes were opened and
I understood nature.'*

Claude Monet

A struggling artist

▲ This photograph shows the dramatic effects of light on the colour of snow, effects that Monet captures in his painting *The Magpie* (opposite).

COLOURS OF SNOW

Of all the seasons, Monet loved painting the sights and shades of winter best of all.

Unlike many traditional artists who painted snow as pure white with grey in the shadows, Monet used the jewel-bright colours he could actually see on a sparkling winter's day.

In the painting opposite, for example, he has added gold, cream, lemon and pink where the sun slants through the trees, and blue, grey and lilac in the shadows of the bush.

Monet's fascination with working in the open air was becoming an obsession. He wanted only to work on outdoor scenes, but landscapes were not popular – especially ones of his colourful, sketchy variety – and he needed money. So he painted anything that he thought would sell. His success at the Salon had been brief and in 1867, 1868 and 1869 all the works he entered were rejected.

BECOMING A FATHER

To add to his money problems, Monet's girlfriend Camille gave birth to their first son, Jean. Monet could not afford to marry Camille because of his family's objections. His father still refused to send him any money or help to support him. Monet and Camille were so poor that at times they could not afford to eat.

◄ *The Luncheon*, Claude Monet, 1868. Camille and Jean are shown here enjoying a hearty lunch, although at the time the Monet family was desperately poor. The food and setting are probably a view of the family life that Monet longed for.

Despite these troubles, Monet continued to visit the Forest of Fontainebleau with his friends whenever he could. Paintings like *The Magpie* (right) show that he was still trying out new ways of capturing what he saw on canvas. This painting was rejected from the Salon, however, in 1869.

TIMELINE ▶

10 June 1867	8 August 1867	May 1868	25 April 1869
Monet travels to Le Havre to stay with Aunt Marie-Jeanne for the summer.	Camille gives birth to a boy. Monet is in Le Havre and cannot afford to go to Paris.	Monet, Camille and Jean move to the country. In despair over money problems, Monet throws himself into the River Seine, but luckily does not drown.	Monet moves with Camille and Jean to the village of Saint-Michel.

The Magpie, 1869

oil on canvas 89 x 130 cm Musée d'Orsay, Paris

Monet used dramatic colours to show the radiance of snow. The black and white magpie on the gate contrasts with the dazzling colours all around and leads our eyes around the painting.

'I am going into the country, which is so lovely now that I almost like it better in winter than in summer.'

Claude Monet

Moving to London

In the summer of 1870 Monet married Camille. When war broke out between France and Prussia in July that year, Monet left his wife and child and went to England to avoid having to join the army and fight. However, though Monet begged him not to, his friend Frédéric Bazille did volunteer and was killed early in the war.

▲ *A Winter's Day in Piccadilly, London*, Von Giuseppe de Niffis, 1875. Many European artists were working in London during the 1870s.

LIFE IN LONDON

In London (where Camille and Jean later joined him), Monet met up with the artists Camille Pissarro (1830-1903) and Alfred Sisley (1839-99) who had also escaped the fighting. Together the friends visited galleries and museums, studying the works of Constable and Turner.

Monet painted many London scenes, including the parks and *The Thames Below Westminster* (right) in 1871. The friends met the French art dealer, Paul Durand-Ruel, who liked their work and bought some of their paintings.

LONDON IN THE 1870S

London in the 1870s was one of the world's largest and busiest cities. Streets bustled with shoppers, street-sellers, horse-drawn carriages and bicycles. Trains and steamboats brought ever more people to swell the population of the growing city.

Londoners were proud of their modern metropolis. Music halls, pleasure parks, theatres, museums and galleries attracted visitors from all over the world.

Beneath the city, people flocked to travel on the world's first underground trains and, at night, electric lamps in the streets replaced the dingy gaslights.

TIMELINE ▶

28 June 1870	19 July 1870	September 1870	18 November 1870	Late November 1870	January 1871
Monet marries Camille. Her family gives her a small dowry.	France declares war on Prussia.	Monet travels to London to escape the Franco-Prussian war. About two weeks later Camille and Jean join him.	Frédéric Bazille is killed in action.	Monet meets art dealer, Paul Durand-Ruel. He selects one of Monet's paintings for exhibition.	Monet paints views of London.

The Thames Below Westminster, 1871

oil on canvas 47 x 72.5 cm National Gallery, London

In this picture Monet painted some of London's newest buildings. The Houses of Parliament (Westminster) had been rebuilt in 1847 after being gutted by a fire in 1834; Big Ben was completed in 1858 and Westminster Bridge had opened in 1862. The men in the picture are demolishing a jetty that had been used to construct the Victoria Embankment. Monet painted the picture from another jetty.

'Monet and I were very enthusiastic about the London landscapes... We worked from nature.'

Camille Pissarro

The Franco-Prussian War

◄ *The Siege of Paris*, Ernest Meissonier, 1871. Parisian civilians suffered terribly when the Prussians besieged the city.

In 1852 Napoleon III (the nephew of Napoleon Bonaparte) became Emperor of France. His rule was known as the Second Empire.

But the balance of power in Europe was shifting – Prussia was gradually emerging as the dominant force among the many principalities that then made up Germany. Under the control of its chancellor, Otto Von Bismarck, Prussia was slowly uniting Germany into a single nation. France, a major power in Europe, felt itself threatened.

THE TURNING POINT

Matters came to a head in 1870, when Bismarck tried to put a German prince on the throne of Spain. This angered the French foreign minister, who accused the Prussians of trying to upset the balance of power.

In July 1870, France declared war on Prussia. Although the war was declared by France, Prussia had cleverly planned it. It led to disaster for France – and Germany officially becoming one united country.

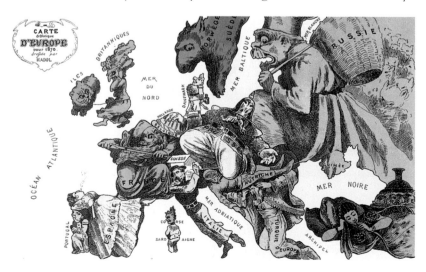

► This woodcut, produced just before the outbreak of the Franco-Prussian War, shows the countries of Europe at the time as different characters.

FRANCE'S DEFEAT

During August 1870 the French army suffered several defeats. In September, in Sedan in north-east France, it was completely defeated. Napoleon III was taken prisoner, the Second Empire ended and France was a republic again.

THE FALL OF PARIS

In September, the Prussians besieged Paris; two million people faced hunger and disease. In 1871, an armistice was signed and, in March, the Prussians left. Because France had lost the war, it was forced to pay five billion francs to Prussia and to give them most of Alsace-Lorraine, an area important for its iron ore and coal.

THE COMMUNE

Before long, fighting broke out again in Paris. This time it was civil war.

Some were angry that France had surrendered to Prussia and felt that the new government, based at Versailles, favoured the rich. Elections were held for a separate government, the Commune, which declared it was in charge of Paris.

The Commune, however, was not accepted by the government at Versailles. The regular army forced its way into the city and the fighting was fiercer than the battles with Prussia. The Commune was defeated but the army killed over 20,000 people – more than had died in the war against Prussia.

THE EFFECT ON MONET

By the time Monet returned to Paris in late 1871, people wanted a more traditional style of art. New ways of painting were rejected in favour of art showing heroic stories that the nation could feel proud about. This made it hard for Monet and his friends to earn a living selling the sort of paintings they were doing at the time.

▲ A photograph taken in 1871, during the Paris Commune, showing a street barricade.

Returning to France

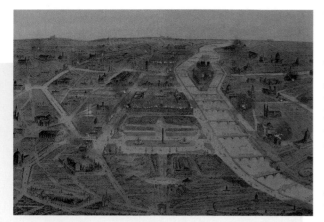

▲ A view of Paris in 1871.
This painting shows the extent of the damage following the Franco-Prussian War and the Commune.

THE DESTRUCTION OF PARIS

It's not surprising that Monet avoided Paris when he returned to France with his family. After the many terrible events, Paris was devastated. Thousands of people had been killed, bridges and buildings had been destroyed and rubble filled the streets.

But early in 1872, engineers, builders, officials and the general public all pulled together to rebuild their capital. Some twenty years earlier, Paris had been transformed from a dirty, medieval city into a gleaming modern metropolis with cafés, restaurants, parks, squares, churches and theatres.

The French were determined to regain that splendour.

In January 1871, Monet heard that his father had died. Although he had inherited some money, he did not return to France, but remained in London in order to avoid the troubles in Paris. The family left London in late May. They travelled through Holland first, staying in a place called Zaandam, where Monet painted several pictures.

ARGENTEUIL

By November 1871 they were back in Paris, which was severely damaged. They did not stay long but moved to Argenteuil (see map on page 7), a pretty town on the banks of the River Seine where they rented a house. Monet experimented with painting yachts, railways, flowers, figures and the effects of light on water. He painted daily from the riverbank or from his floating studio boat. *Regatta at Argenteuil* (right) was painted at this time.

▲ *Monet in his Floating Studio*, Edouard Manet, 1874.

TIMELINE ▶

17 January 1871	Late May 1871	November 1871	End of 1871	January 1872	June 1872	1872–1874
Monet's father, Adolphe, dies. Monet inherits some money.	Monet and family leave England for Holland.	The family returns to Paris.	The family moves to Argenteuil.	The rebuilding of Paris begins.	Durand-Ruel buys 25 of Monet's pictures.	Monet paints in Argenteuil, often from his floating studio.

Regatta at Argenteuil, 1872

oil on canvas 48 x 75 cm Musée d'Orsay, Paris

Monet's love of water never left him. Here, he does not paint every ripple, but uses just a few brushstrokes and firm slabs of colour where he can see the reflections. Nothing is blended to look realistic, but the bold, clear colours show the bright stillness of the day.

'This is a man who will be greater than any of us. Buy his work.'

Charles-François Daubigny (1817-78), French landscape painter

'Impressionism' is born

PAINTING MODERN LIFE

Monet lived through a time of great industrial change. New machines made life easier, but they were also ugly and created a lot of smoke and dirt. Traditional artists would not paint them.

So when Monet painted railway bridges, the effects of smoke in the air and people in modern-day dress, he was once again going against traditional art. This shocked people, though Monet maintained he was being honest in painting what he saw.

▲ The first 'Impressionist' exhibition was held in a photographer's studio in the Boulevard des Capucines (above). It cost one franc to enter. People flocked in, mainly to laugh at the brightly coloured and sketchy paintings.

▲ Monet was not afraid to capture the realities of industrialised France, such as the effects of smoke on the Paris skyline.

In 1874, unhappy about being rejected by the Salon, Monet and his friends decided to hold an independent exhibition. Twenty-nine artists, including Monet, Camille Pissarro, Alfred Sisley, Auguste Renoir, Paul Cézanne, Edgar Degas, Edouard Manet and Johan Jongkind exhibited for a month, just before the Salon, in an empty photographer's studio.

The exhibition was not a success, although it did bring attention to the artists. People came mainly to laugh. A critic, Louis Leroy, wrote an insulting article 'Exhibition of Impressionists' after seeing Monet's *Impression, Sunrise* (right). He accused them of making mud-splashes, not paintings! Others quickly adopted the name 'Impressionists' and the artists themselves agreed that it suited their work.

Two years later, when the Impressionists exhibited at the house of the art dealer Paul Durand-Ruel, people still scoffed at their sketchy style, their industrial landscapes and their images of Parisian life, though the press were a little kinder.

TIMELINE ▶

January 1873	15 April 1874	24 April 1874	Early 1875	March 1875	April 1876
Monet stays in Le Havre and paints seascapes.	Monet and his friends hold their first exhibition.	Louis Leroy's scornful article 'Exhibition of Impressionists' is published.	Facing financial problems, Monet and his family move to a smaller house.	Monet and his friends auction some paintings, but earn little from this.	The second Impressionist exhibition is organised at Paul Durand-Ruel's house.

Impression, Sunrise, 1872–3

oil on canvas 48 x 63 cm Musée Marmottan, Paris

Monet always maintained that this picture was not meant to be an accurate view of the port of Le Havre, but a view of the changing light. The picture records a mood, not a scene. Monet painted it from his hotel window during a stay there in 1873. It was exhibited at the first 'Impressionist' exhibition in 1874.

'… something I did at Le Havre: the sun in the mist, and a few ships' masts… I said, "Call it Impression".'

Claude Monet

Understanding colour

For Monet and his friends, colour was the most important aspect of their work. Traditionally, drawing the picture had been as important as the added colour, but because the Impressionists worked quickly, they had no need to begin with a detailed picture. In addition, the colours available to artists were increasing.

Until the nineteenth century the pigments (paint colours) artists were able to use had been very limited. Then new chemical and dyeing techniques suddenly allowed painters an explosion of new colours. At last, artists could produce the vivid tones of nature, such as brilliant sunlight or shimmering sea.

◀ After the 1840s, oil paints were stored in small metal tubes with lids. Artists no longer had to worry that the paint would dry up. They could pack their bags and go off painting whenever and wherever they liked.

PORTABLE PAINTS

Originally, paints had to be mixed from powder, which was messy and time-consuming. But by the mid-1800s, oil paints were sold ready-mixed in metal tubes, making them portable for painting trips. For the first time, artists could leave their studios and paint when and where they liked. The Impressionists took advantage of this, painting pure colours directly on to their canvases, creating dazzling effects.

'Colours in tubes allowed us to paint totally from nature. Without colours in tubes, there would be no Cézanne, no Monet, no Pissarro and no Impressionism.'

Auguste Renoir (1841-1919)

Monet's painting *Impression, Sunrise* (reproduced on the previous page) appears hazy because of the way Monet used oil paints. He did not think of what he was painting, only of what he actually saw and especially of the blocks of colours he saw.

▲ *Portrait of Claude Monet*, Auguste Renoir, 1875. This painting shows Monet at work by a window. On his palette are daubs of coloured paints. He uses several different brushes for the one painting.

THE IMPRESSIONIST PALETTE

The Impressionists used contrasting colours for shadows – not simply black and white. This made their pictures appear brighter than work by earlier artists. However, it was not entirely their own idea. The Impressionists' use of colour was also influenced by scientific discoveries.

SCIENTIFIC THEORIES

In the mid-19th century, scientists began developing new theories about colour. Contemporary artists may not have understood the theories but, consciously or unconsciously, they put them into practice.

Artists such as Monet were interested in the quality of light and the way the eye sees. They understood that shadow is never just black or grey, but coloured. They also realised that the colour of the light changes the colour of objects. For example, a haystack is yellow, but in different lights it can appear gold, blue or even red.

Monet shows this beautifully in his painting *Haystacks at the End of Summer, Morning* (see page 29).

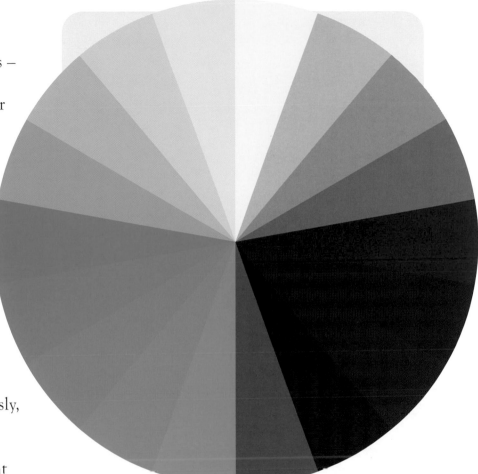

▲ In 1666, the scientist Sir Isaac Newton (1642-1727) discovered that in what we see as white light there are seven colours: red, orange, yellow, green, blue, indigo and violet.

In the mid-nineteenth century, a chemist, Eugène Chevreul, wrote a book about colours. He designed this colour wheel to show the relationship between the colours that Newton had discovered. 'Cool' colours such as blue, appear to sink back, while 'warm' colours' such as red, appear to come forward.

Colours that are opposite to each other on the wheel look brighter when they are together – for example, red and green, or blue and yellow. These are called complementary colours. Monet put complementary colours alongside each other in many of his paintings.

HOW WE SEE COLOUR

Scientists discovered that we all see colours differently and that opposite, or complementary colours appear brighter when placed next to each other. Monet probably worked this out for himself. He used a rich palette with many colours and, from the 1870s, avoided black as much as possible.

An industrial world

▲ The first railway in France was opened in 1828. Within just a few years steam locomotives had replaced horsepower as the main means of travel.

Paris had its first railway in 1837, and by 1841 there were 560 kilometres of railway across France.

MODERNISATION

By the late 1870s the impact of modernisation was being felt all around the world.

Railways were spreading across countries like spider's webs, linking different places and making it possible to work in one place and live in another. In France, the newly-built railway stations were nicknamed 'palaces of modern industry'.

The Impressionists themselves regularly travelled by train to visit the countryside around Paris.

In Monet's time railways were changing society – day trips could be enjoyed without the expense of a full holiday. Monet was fascinated by one of Paris's main railway stations, the Gare Saint-Lazare, and used it in a series of paintings. At the third Impressionist exhibition, he displayed seven views of the station alongside other works. Such industrial scenes were unusual at the time, but Monet's series portrayed the mood and energy of the busy station most effectively.

THE RISE OF IMPRESSIONISM

In 1878, Monet's second son, Michel, was born. Later that year Monet and his family moved to Vétheuil (see map, page 7), a village on the Seine near Paris, to live with Ernest and Alice Hoschedé and their children. Monet painted around the village and the riverbank. To make money he also painted still-lifes as they sold more easily than landscapes.

Towards the end of the 1870s, Impressionist paintings were beginning to become more popular. The art dealer Paul Durand-Ruel, in particular, was very active in promoting them. Between 1878 and 1879 Monet exhibited at another two Impressionist exhibitions.

In 1879 Camille died after a long illness.

◄ *Purple Poppies*, Claude Monet, 1879. This is one of the still-life paintings that Monet produced to earn money during Camille's illness.

TIMELINE ▶

January 1877	5 April 1877	17 March 1878	August 1878	10 April 1879	5 September 1879
Monet begins painting at the Gare Saint-Lazare.	Third Impressionist exhibition.	Monet's second son, Michel, is born. Camille falls ill.	The Monets move to Vétheuil to live with Ernest and Alice Hoschedé and their six children.	Fourth Impressionist exhibition. Monet exhibits 29 paintings.	Camille dies.

Interior of the Gare Saint-Lazare, 1877

oil on canvas 54.3 x 73.6 cm National Gallery, London

Monet was enchanted by the light pouring through the glass and steel roof of this Paris station and by the colours in the clouds of steam escaping from the trains. He painted twelve pictures of this same subject, each one different to the last.

'These great-glassed-in workshops, like Saint-Lazare... which spread above this gutted city like immense skies.'

Marcel Proust (1871-1922), French novelist

The search for inspiration

▲ Monet's house at Giverny.

REJECTING THE SALON

Despite the Impressionists' independent exhibitions, acceptance by the Paris Salon continued to be a vital factor for an artist's financial success.

By 1880, although Monet was becoming quite well known for his original style of painting, he still needed publicity to sell his work. So he was pleased to be accepted for the 1880 Salon, although some of his artist friends thought he was going against their independent standpoint.

In 1881, Paul Durand-Ruel agreed to buy almost all of Monet's paintings. Monet, at last, no longer needed to face rejection at the Salon, and he turned his back on it forever.

After the death of Camille, Monet and his sons remained in the house at Vétheuil with Alice Hoschedé and her children. Alice had nursed Camille through her illness, looking after Jean and Michel as well as her own six children, and helping to pay off Monet's debts. It was here Monet painted *Artist's Garden* (right).

◀ *The Painter Claude Monet*, Gustave Caillebotte, 1884. Here, Monet is shown walking in the quiet village of Giverny, about 85 kilometres from Paris.

In December 1881, Monet moved with Alice and the children to Poissy, near Paris. Soon they all moved again, to Giverny (see map page 7), further along the Seine. They rented a house with a garden, near a stream.

TRAVELLING FOR INSPIRATION

Monet complained to the art dealer Paul Durand-Ruel that he needed inspiration. In December 1883, he set off with Auguste Renoir on a painting trip to the South of France and the Italian Riviera. Between 1883 and 1885 he travelled even more in search of interesting landscapes.

TIMELINE ▶

1 April 1880	1 May 1880	June 1880	February 1881	March 1881	December 1881	Spring 1882	29 April 1883
Monet does not exhibit at the 5th Impressionist exhibition.	Monet enters two paintings for the Salon. One accepted.	Monet has his first one-man show.	Monet decides not to enter for the Salon again.	Monet does not exhibit at the 6th Impressionist exhibition.	Monet, Alice and the children move to Poissy.	Monet exhibits at the 7th Impressionist exhibition.	Monet, Alice and the children move to Giverny.

The Artist's Garden at Vétheuil, 1880

oil on canvas 151.4 x 121 cm National Gallery of Art, Washington

Monet loved both flowers and his children. Here he contrasts his two small children and Alice, all dressed in white, with the tall, brilliantly-coloured flowers.

Success at last

By holding their own exhibitions away from the Salon, Monet and his friends changed the way people viewed art. The eighth and final Impressionist exhibition was held in June 1886, but Monet did not take part. During the 1880s, there were frequent shows of his paintings, not only in France but all around the world. In 1889 Monet and other Impressionists exhibited at the Exposition Universelle in Paris. Later that year Monet shared an exhibition with the sculptor Auguste Rodin (1840-1917). It was a great success. In 1890 he could afford to buy the house at Giverny.

▲ *Claude Monet Painting by the Edge of a Wood,* John Singer Sargent, 1885. Monet is seen here with Alice Hoschedé's daughter, Blanche, in a meadow behind the house at Giverny.

▲ Monet's beautiful garden at Giverny provided him with plenty of opportunity to explore light and colour.

PAINTING THE LIGHT

Monet had always been interested in the changes to atmosphere and light. In Giverny, he developed this further. He would paint out in the open air, then complete the colourful pictures in his studio. He would paint a scene at different times of the day and year to capture on canvas the differing effects of the light.

SERIES PAINTINGS

Throughout his career, Monet had painted repeated versions of the same subject.

By the 1890s, he had developed this into his 'series' paintings, working for a few minutes at a time on the same image at different times of the day and in different weather conditions. He worked quickly on each canvas – capturing a moment, showing how light changes colours and creates atmosphere.

His first series featured haystacks, one of which is shown on the right.

TIMELINE ▶

March 1886	June 1886	15 June 1886	April 1889	June 1889	Autumn 1890	November 1890	4 May 1891
40 Monet works are exhibited in the USA.	The 8th and final Impressionist exhibition.	Monet exhibits 13 paintings at an International Exhibition.	The Exposition Universelle, Paris.	Monet shares a major exhibition with Auguste Rodin.	Monet begins working on his series of haystack paintings.	Monet buys the house in Giverny.	Durand-Ruel has a one-man exhibition of Monet's works.

Haystacks at the End of Summer, Morning, 1891

oil on canvas 60.5 x 100.5 cm Musée d'Orsay, Paris

These haystacks were in a field near Monet's house in Giverny. He painted them 25 times
between the end of summer and the coming of winter, sometimes from different angles,
in bright colours and bathed in glowing light.

*'Forget what is before you – a tree, a house, a field –
and think simply: here's a small blue square,
there's a pink rectangle, there's a yellow band,
then paint it as you see it.'*

Claude Monet

'La Belle France'

By the late 1880s, the Franco-Prussian War and the Commune were a distant memory. In spring 1889, Paris held an Exposition Universelle (World Fair). This was a huge exhibition to mark 100 years since the French Revolution, and to show off some of France's most important achievements.

World fairs were very popular during the second half of the 19th century. They were held in many different countries, and other nations were invited to exhibit as well. Most countries wanted to impress others, and a great deal of money was spent building pavilions and filling them with examples of scientific, technical and artistic accomplishments.

In Paris in 1889, the development of electricity, engineering skills and creativity were some of the main achievements that France wanted to display.

▲ The French car manufacturer, Louis Renault, demonstrates one of the first cars, c. 1898.

▲ The Eiffel Tower under construction, 1880s. It was built to last just 20 years.

THE EIFFEL TOWER

As an attraction for the Exposition Universelle, the engineer Gustave Eiffel (1832-1923) built a tall, slim iron tower to demonstrate the progress of 19th-century French engineering. In the shape of a huge capital A, the Eiffel Tower's foundations went 15 metres underground and it rose 300 metres above ground. For 40 years, it was the tallest structure in the world.

Visitors could climb to the top, and stop at different levels to enjoy the view across Paris. One section had engravings with the names of great people in French history. At first, many Parisians complained that it was ugly and spoiled the look of Paris, but it soon became an unmistakable symbol of the city.

▲ People flocked to see the illuminated fountain at the Exposition Universelle, 1889.

ELECTRICITY

Over 25 million visitors to the Exposition Universelle witnessed the marvels of electricity. Gas lighting was weak and dingy, but the electric beacon at the top of the Eiffel Tower could be seen 112 kilometres away. Searchlights on the tower picked out buildings some nine kilometres away, right on the outskirts of Paris. And at the Telephone Pavilion visitors listened to singers performing at the Opéra, a taste of radio broadcasts to come.

Machinery Hall, a huge iron and glass building 420 metres long, with a 115-metre roof span, proudly demonstrated French construction skills. Inside, two movable bridges raised visitors to the level of the machinery being exhibited. Machinery Hall alone was lit by 20,000 electric lamps.

ART SECTION

The art section of the Exposition Universelle contained many impressive exhibits, including several of the latest works from Claude Monet, Edouard Manet (1832-83), and Camille Pissarro (1830-1903).

◀ Some of the world's first electric lightbulbs were demonstrated at the Exposition Universelle in Paris.

Rouen and Norway

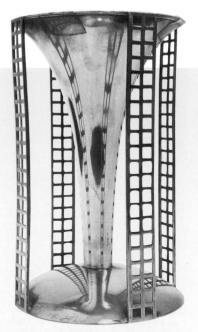

▲ This vase was designed by Josef Hoffmann, an Austrian architect and designer of interiors, furniture and decorative objects. He was one of the pioneers in the new, modern architecture and design that came in during the 1890s.

A NEW STYLE

Gustave Eiffel's tower made entirely of iron symbolised the modern era. Throughout the world, artists, architects and designers were creating new designs using new, modern materials.

In the 1890s two shops, Art Nouveau in Paris and Liberty in London, sold modern and Oriental art. They lent their names to the new style, called 'Art Nouveau' in England and 'Style Liberty' in France.

At last, changes and new ideas were becoming acceptable, and Monet's work no longer seemed as strange.

In 1892 Monet travelled to Rouen in Normandy. He wanted to create a series of paintings of the famous cathedral. First he set up his easel in a shop, then in an apartment opposite the cathedral. He painted it for half an hour then changed his canvas and painted it again. Each painting shows the same building but in different colours – purple and yellow, gold and pink, blue and bronze.

Later that year, after the death of her husband, Monet married Alice Hoschedé.

NORWEGIAN LANDSCAPES

In the winter of 1894-5, Monet visited his stepson in Norway. He loved the dramatic scenery and snow and set about painting them. On his return to France, Paul Durand-Ruel exhibited 20 of Monet's cathedral paintings and eight Norwegian landscapes. The show was a huge success. By now his reputation had grown and his money worries were behind him.

▲ The dramatic landscapes and colours of Norway inspired Monet when he visited the country in 1895.

TIMELINE ▶

February 1892	16 July 1892	February 1893	January-April 1895	May 1896
Monet begins the Rouen Cathedral series.	Monet and Alice get married.	Monet returns to Rouen to paint once more. He keeps returning until 1895.	Monet paints landscapes in Norway.	An exhibition of the Rouen Cathedral series is extremely successful.

Rouen Cathedral in Full Sunlight, 1894
oil on canvas 107 x 73 cm Musée d'Orsay, Paris
Monet painted 30 versions of this building, Rouen Cathedral, showing it in different weather conditions and times of day. The thick layers of paint really look like stone walls shimmering in the sunlight.

Living in style

In 1900 Monet had an eye accident that forced him to stop work for a time. This marked the beginning of many years of eye problems.

His eyesight weakened in 1908 and, by about 1915, he had begun to lose the ability to see colour. All colours seemed tinted reddish-brown. Only in 1923, after several operations and with a special pair of glasses, did his eyesight improve.

The years of failing eyesight caused Monet much grief. Two of his artist friends, Edgar Degas (1834-1917) and Mary Cassatt (1844-1926), had already gone blind. Monet was sure that he too would become blind.

▲ In 1901 Queen Victoria died, aged 82. Although Monet could speak very little English, he enjoyed being a tourist and watched the funeral procession from a friend's house. He described what he saw as 'a unique spectacle'.

Monet spent much time developing his garden at Giverny. He planted vegetables, fruit trees and flowers everywhere. By redirecting part of a nearby river, he enlarged his pond, then planted water-lilies and grew trailing plants and trees all around it. He added a Japanese-style footbridge over the pond – a simple arch in his favourite shade of green.

▲ *Savoy Hotel,* Harold Oakley, c. 1889. Monet and Alice stayed here on the sixth floor in 1899.

VISITING LONDON

In September 1899, Monet and Alice visited London. They could now afford to stay at the Savoy, a new luxury hotel, for six weeks. Monet returned, alone, in 1900 and 1901, for three months at a time. He painted three separate series of the River Thames – views of Charing Cross Bridge, Waterloo Bridge and the Houses of Parliament. The bridges were painted from his balcony at the Savoy, and the Houses of Parliament from a nearby hospital.

TIMELINE ▶

Summer 1899	September 1899	December 1900	24 January 1901	2 February 1901	Early 1902
Monet begins the water-lily paintings.	Monet begins the new series of paintings of the River Thames in London.	Back in France, an eye accident forces Monet to stop work.	Monet returns to London to continue his Thames series.	Monet watches Queen Victoria's funeral procession.	Durand-Ruel has a solo exhibition of Monet's work in the USA.

London, The Houses of Parliament. Sunshine Through the Fog, 1900-4

oil on canvas 81 x 92 cm Musée d'Orsay, Paris

London fascinated Monet, especially the River Thames. This painting shows how his technique has developed since his earlier London work (see page 15), where the shapes are more defined. Here, he has painted the hazy effects of fog, creating atmosphere – using swirls of glowing colour and rippled reflections in the water.

'Every day I find London more beautiful to paint.'

Claude Monet

Monet's garden

It took six full-time gardeners to help Monet develop his garden. He worked on it too, designing it like a painting with areas of light and shade, and harmonious colours.

From the early 1900s, the pond became Monet's favourite place to paint, and it continued to occupy him for the next 25 years. His paintings became larger, and if anything even more 'Impressionist'. In 1914 Monet had a third studio built in the garden to allow him to work on a huge scale.

MADRID AND VENICE

In 1904, flushed with the success of his London series, Monet bought a car and drove Alice and Michel to Madrid for a holiday. In 1908 he and Alice visited Venice and, fascinated by the light, Monet painted several views of it.

Soon after their return, however, Alice fell ill and died. Three years later, his son Jean died. Some of Monet's friends were also dead, his eyesight was failing and World War I (1914-18) had begun.

Monet was deeply unhappy and now rarely left Giverny, concentrating on tending and painting his garden.

▲ *Footbridge Over River with Wisteria in Foreground in Full Bloom*, Ando or Utagawa Hiroshige, c. 1840. This is a typical Japanese colour woodblock print.

◄ Venice has inspired artists for centuries. During his visit, Monet was always on the lookout for suitable spots to set up his easel and paint.

THE INFLUENCE OF JAPAN

In the 1850s Japanese prints started being sold in France for the first time. They became very popular, and were collected by many people including Monet.

Japanese artists liked to balance their pictures with calm and busy areas, unusual viewpoints and flat decoration.

Many of Monet's paintings and parts of his garden were clearly inspired by Japanese art.

TIMELINE ▶

Spring 1904	October 1904	Spring 1908	September 1908	May-June 1909	19 May 1911	10 February 1914
Success of Monet's London series. He buys a car!	Monet drives to Madrid with Alice and Michel.	Monet's eyesight weakens.	Monet and Alice visit Venice. They stay for over two months.	Durand-Ruel shows 48 pictures from Monet's water-lily series.	Alice dies. Monet's eyesight weakens further.	Monet's eldest son, Jean, dies after a long illness.

Water-lilies, 1903

oil on canvas Private Collection, Tokyo

From the early 1900s Monet spent most of his time painting the water garden at Giverny.
Monet's weeping willows can be seen as a shadowy reflection in the deep blue water.

'... then suddenly it dawned on me how wonderful
my pond was, and I reached for my palette.'

Claude Monet

A gift for France

OPENING OF THE ORANGERIE

The Musée de l'Orangerie can be found in the Jardin des Tuileries, a park in central Paris. In two enormous oval rooms, Monet's twelve vast canvases, commissioned by Prime Minister Clemenceau, cover the walls.

The paintings are not like Monet's earlier Impressionist works – they are bigger, less clearly defined and do not show complete 'scenes'. Yet his fascination for water, flowers, reflections and the open air are still very much in evidence.

Sadly, Monet did not live to see the unveiling of his paintings there in 1927.

▲ A photograph of Monet at Giverny, beside his Japanese bridge.

▲ Monet's paintings of the *Nymphéas* (water-lilies) are displayed in two large rooms at the Musée de l'Orangerie, Paris.
This photograph was taken in 1930, but the exhibition is still there today.

In 1914 Georges Clemenceau, the French Prime Minister and a friend of Monet, asked him to paint some water-lilies as a gift for France. Monet decided to donate two water-lily paintings, but Clemenceau wanted to create a massive decorative area dedicated to the glory of France. After years of discussion over Monet's payment and also his loss of confidence (he could now barely see), the pictures were eventually finished and are on display at the Orangerie in Paris.

MONET'S FINAL YEARS

Even with failing eyesight Monet painted many inspirational works such as *The Weeping Willow* (right). After two eye operations in 1923, and a special pair of glasses, his eyesight slowly improved.

Monet spent the last years of his life painting his pond, the water-lilies and weeping willows from his third large studio in Giverny. He had become one of France's most famous and important artists. On 5 December 1926, he died at Giverny, aged 86.

TIMELINE ▶

Spring 1914	3 August 1914	1918	January-July 1923	September 1923	5 December 1926
Monet begins his large-scale pictures for the nation.	World War I begins. Michel Monet is called up for military service.	Monet completes eight water-lily decorations. His eyesight worsens. World War I ends.	Monet has three eye operations.	Monet is given special glasses and his eyesight improves.	Monet dies at Giverny, aged 86.

The Weeping Willow, 1921–22

oil on canvas 116 x 89 cm Musée Marmottan, Paris

When he painted this Monet could scarcely see. Instead of his usual soft, brightly-coloured paints, he used colours that were much darker and heavier in tone.

Monet's legacy

At first they were laughed at, but within his lifetime, Monet's paintings became some of the most popular in the world. By 1891, his reputation had grown so much that an exhibition of his paintings at Paul Durand-Ruel's gallery in Paris sold out within just three days of opening.

COLOUR AND SUBJECT

By painting the effects of light, Monet explored colour in a way that few artists had previously attempted. He also painted views as he saw them, without changing them in any way to make them more acceptable to the viewer. He believed this was honest and that he was being true to nature.

OPENING THE WAY

Their dedication to this new style of painting, despite the harsh criticism, has meant that Monet and the other Impressionists have added new traditions to the old ones. They claimed the right for every artist to paint as he or she chooses, and this has had a huge effect on the art that has developed since.

▲ *Irises*, Vincent van Gogh, 1889.

FOLLOWING MONET

Monet's energetic and colourful works have inspired many other artists. Vincent van Gogh (1853-90) changed from using dark colours to bright ones after meeting Monet and discussing Impressionist theories. He admired Monet's use of pure, brilliant colours and bold brush-strokes, and the way he painted out in the open air directly from nature.

As a young man Henri Matisse (1869-1954) painted in the Impressionist style. He developed his love of colour partly through looking at Monet's bright colours and free style. He learned a lot from Monet's paintings about using dashes of colour to give the impression of sparkling light.

Although their styles are different, it was Monet's free use of colour that inspired Matisse's bright, bold images.

▲ *The Open Window*, Henri Matisse, 1905.

▲ The Musée Marmottan in Paris.

MUSÉE MARMOTTAN

The largest collection of works by Claude Monet can be found in the Musée Marmottan, in Paris. This is largely thanks to Madame Donop de Monchy, the daughter of Monet's friend Georges de Bellio, and Michel Monet, the painter's younger son.

Housed in a specially-built hall, the collection offers a unique opportunity to see major works from the various stages of Monet's career, and therefore to follow the development of his style. It begins with the Le Havre caricatures of c.1858, and continues right through to paintings inspired by the garden at Giverny.

Included are scenes of the Normandy coast, the Houses of Parliament in London, and the famous picture that gave Impressionism its name: *Impression: Sunrise* (page 21).

Good friends

All great artists develop their style through a combination of their own ideas and learning from others. Monet was good friends with many artists and learned a lot from them. One of his closest friends was Camille Pissarro (1830-1903) whom he first met at the Académie Suisse in 1859. Pissarro, along with Alfred Sisley and Auguste Renoir, believed in the same ideas as Monet and formed the core of the Impressionists.

ESCAPE!

In 1870-71 Monet and Pissarro were delighted to meet up in London, where they had fled from the Franco-Prussian war, and spent a lot of time together.

Monet and I were very enthusiastic about the London landscapes…We worked from nature… We also visited the museums.

▲ Pissarro, writing to his son Lucien in 1900, remembered his stay in London in 1870-71.

It is good to draw everything and anything. When you have trained yourself to see a tree truly, you know how to look at the human figure. Specialisation is not necessary.

▲ Part of another letter to Lucien, dated 25 July 1883. Ten years earlier, Pissarro had written: '[Monet's] is a highly conscious art, based upon observation… It is poetry through the harmony of true colours. Monet adores real nature.'

SIDE-BY-SIDE

Back in Paris, Pissarro and Monet often painted together and, sitting drinking at the Café Guerbois, discussed how to capture 'the impression of nature'. In 1874, they both exhibited at the photographer's studio where they gained the nickname 'Impressionists'. Pissarro went on to exhibit at all eight of the Impressionist exhibitions, although Monet only exhibited at five.

The two artists agreed on many things, such as painting just what they saw before them, painting in the open air, using short brushstrokes of pure, bright colours and rarely using black or brown. They also had the same ideas about developing artistic skill.

TIMELINE ▶

1840	1859	1865	1871	1877	1880
1840 Oscar-Claude Monet is born on 14 November in Paris.	**1859** Joins the Académie Suisse and meets Camille Pissarro.	**1865** Meets Camille Doncieux.	**1871** Father dies. The Prussian war ends. Visits Holland then returns to Paris. Moves to Argenteuil.	**1877** Paints the Gare Sainte-Lazare and exhibits at the third Impressionist exhibition.	**1880** Does not exhibit in the fifth Impressionist exhibition, but one of his paintings is accepted at the Salon and he has his first one-man exhibition.
1845 Moves to Le Havre.	**1861** Conscripted into the French army and goes to Algeria.	**1866** The Salon accepts three Monet paintings.	**1874** Monet and friends hold their own exhibition.	**1878** Michel is born. Moves to Vétheuil with the Hoschedés.	**1881** He does not enter the sixth Impressionist show. Moves to Poissy.
1857 Mother dies.	**1862** Monet is ill with typhoid, returns to Le Havre. Returns to Paris to enter Charles Gleyre's studio.	**1867** Jean, Monet's first son, is born.	**1876** Exhibits at the second Impressionist exhibition.	**1879** Exhibits at the fourth Impressionist exhibition. Camille dies.	
1858 Sells his caricatures. Eugène Boudin advises him about painting.		**1870** Marries Camille. Goes to London to escape the Franco-Prussian war, meets Durand-Ruel.			

COMPANIONSHIP

Although Pissarro was ten years older than Monet, they became good friends with each other's families as well as being painting companions.

Thank you again, dear friend, and your wife, for all your kindness and trust in my sincere friendship.

◀ **When Monet's wife died in 1879, Pissarro wrote in sympathy. This is part of Monet's reply to him.**

SERIES PAINTINGS

As time went by, both men developed similar new ideas. By the 1880s, they were both fascinated by the concept of painting a series showing the same scene in different lights and weather conditions.

I have just concluded my series of paintings… Painting, art in general, delights me. It is my life, what else matters? When you put all your soul into a work, you cannot fail to find a kindred soul who understands you.

▲ In 1883 Pissarro wrote this about his own work, which was developing along similar lines to Monet's at the time.

CAMILLE PISSARRO

Camille Pissarro was born in the French West Indies in 1830. He went to school in France, and moved there permanently in 1855. His early art was inspired by Realism and he exhibited at the official Salon in the 1860s. But at the same time, alongside Monet, Renoir and Sisley, he was developing Impressionist techniques.

In the 1870s, at Pontoise, north-east of Paris, he began to paint peasant life. He started his series paintings in the 1880s.

Pissarro only became famous in his 60s, by which time he was dividing his time between the countryside and Paris. He died in 1903 at the age of 73.

▲ *Self-portrait,* Camille Pissarro, 1873.

1882	1890	1893	1900	1908	1918
1882 Exhibits at the seventh Impressionist exhibition.	**1890** Begins working on his series of haystack paintings and buys the house in Giverny.	**1893** Returns to Rouen.	**1900** Back in France, an eye accident forces Monet to stop working for a while.	**1908** Visits Venice.	**1918** Completes eight huge water-lily paintings. End of the First World War.
1883 Moves to Giverny.		**1895** Paints in Norway.		**1909** Exhibits 48 pictures from the water-lily series.	
1886 Does not exhibit at the eighth and final Impressionist exhibition.	**1891** Exhibits 15 haystack paintings at a Durand-Ruel exhibition.	**1896** Cathedral series exhibition is successful.	**1901** Queen Victoria dies. Monet watches her funeral procession.	**1911** Alice dies. Eyesight weakens.	**1923** After three eye operations, eyesight improves.
		1899 Begins his water-lilies and Japanese bridge series. Begins the London series.	**1902** Durand-Ruel has an exhibition of his work in the USA.	**1914** Eldest son, Jean, dies after a long illness. Begins the paintings for France. The First World War begins.	**1926** Dies at Giverny on 5 December, aged 86.
1889 Has a joint exhibition with Auguste Rodin.	**1892** Begins the Rouen Cathedral series. Marries Alice.		**1904** London series is a success.		

Glossary

académie: a place of learning.

Art Nouveau: a decorative style which began about 1890. It was mainly used for ornaments and decoration.

atmosphere: the feeling a place has.

besieged: when an organised group, such as an army, attacks a place and tries to take it over.

canvas: a woven cloth used as a base for paintings. Materials used include linen, cotton and hemp, which are treated to stop the paint sinking too far into the material.

caricature: a cartoon of someone, exaggerating their features to make them look funny.

commission: to place an order for a work of art.

conscription: compulsory service in the armed forces.

dowry: a gift of money for a bride, usually from her family.

easel: a stand for a canvas, so the artist can paint easily.

en plein-air: a French phrase meaning 'in the open air'.

etching: a print on paper made from an engraved metal plate.

exhibition: a public showing of art works.

Impressionists: a group of artists based in Paris during the late 19th century who painted 'impressions' of the world with broad brushstrokes of pure, unmixed colour. The group included Auguste Renoir (1841-1919), Claude Monet (1840-1926) and Edgar Degas (1834-1917).

landscapes: paintings of scenery.

medieval: coming from a time in history called the Middle Ages (c. 1000–1453).

metropolis: a large city.

military service: when someone has to join the armed forces (such as the army) for a set period of time.

modernisation: when things are made modern through the use of technology, such as for transport or in industry.

Norman: relating to the Normans, the people who live in Normandy.

oil paints: thick paints where the colours are mixed with oil.

palette: a flat board on which artists arrange their paints ready for use.

pigment: any substance used to make colours for painting with.

professional artist: an artist who is paid for his work.

reputation: being well thought of, having a good name or being known for good work.

regatta: a sporting event featuring a series of boat or yacht races.

republic: a country where governing power is held by a person or persons elected by the people, not by a monarch.

Salon: annual art exhibition organised by the French Academy. In the 19th century the jury refused works by many Impressionist and Post-Impressionist painters who then exhibited at the Salon des Refusés. The Salon des Independants was started in 1884.

still-life: a picture of objects that do not move, usually carefully arranged by the artist.

studio: an artist's workshop.

tone: in art, the name for the combined effect of the colours and light and dark areas in a picture.

wisteria: a climbing shrub with pale bluish-lilac flowers.

woodblock: a block of wood which is cut into to create a print. The parts that the artist wants to be white are cut away, and then the block is covered with ink and pressed against a sheet of paper.

Museums and galleries

You can see Monet's paintings in art galleries in many different countries around the world. Seeing his works close-up is exciting – you'll be amazed at how many colours he has used! Here is a selected list of galleries and museums that have some of Monet's paintings on display.

Even if you can't visit these galleries yourself, you may be able to visit their websites. Gallery websites often show pictures of the artworks they have on display. Some websites even have virtual tours so that you can wander around while sitting in front of your computer at home or school! Most of the international websites below have an option to view in English.

FRANCE

Musée de l'Orangerie
Jardin des Tuileries
Place de la Concorde, Paris 1

Musée d'Orsay
62 rue de Lille, 75343 Paris, cedex 07
www.musee-orsay.fr

Musée Marmottan
2 rue Louis-Boilly, 75016 Paris
www.marmottan.com

UNITED KINGDOM

Cardiff National Museum & Gallery
Cathays Park, Cardiff, CF10 3NP
www.nmgw.ac.uk

The National Gallery
Trafalgar Square, London WC2N 5DN
www.nationalgallery.org.uk

National Gallery of Scotland
The Mound, Edinburgh EH2 2EL
www.nationalgalleries.org

Tate Modern
Bankside, London
SE1 9TG
www.tate.org.uk/modern

USA

The Art Institute of Chicago
111 South Michigan Avenue
Chicago, Illinois, 60603-6404
www.artic.edu/aic

Museum of Fine Arts, Boston
Avenue of the Arts, 465 Huntington Avenue
Boston, Massachusetts 02115-5523
www.mfa.org

The Metropolitan Museum of Art
1000 Fifth Avenue at 82nd Street, New York
www.metmuseum.org

Museum of Modern Art
11 West 53 Street
New York
NY 10019-5497
www.moma.org

The National Gallery of Art
6th Street and Constitution Avenue, NW,
Washington, DC 20565
www.nga.gov

Philadelphia Museum of Art
Benjamin Franklin Parkway and 26th Street
Philadelphia, PA 19130
www.philamuseum.org

Index